Y0-AGH-333

A LOOK AT CONTINENTS

EXPLORE NORTH AMERICA

by Veronica B. Wilkins

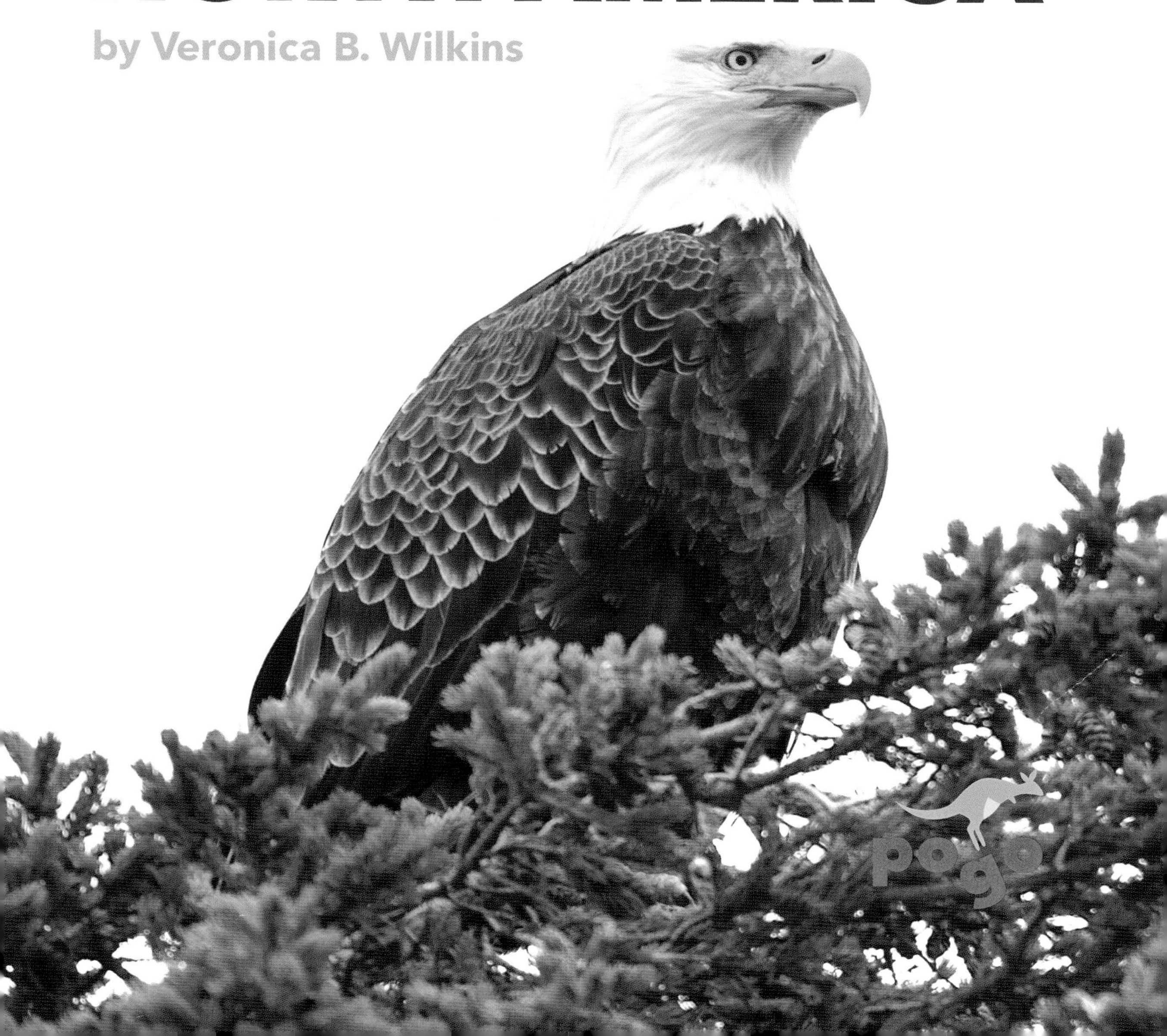

Ideas for Parents and Teachers

Pogo Books let children practice reading informational text while introducing them to nonfiction features such as headings, labels, sidebars, maps, and diagrams, as well as a table of contents, glossary, and index.

Carefully leveled text with a strong photo match offers early fluent readers the support they need to succeed.

Before Reading

- "Walk" through the book and point out the various nonfiction features. Ask the student what purpose each feature serves.
- Look at the glossary together. Read and discuss the words.

Read the Book

- Have the child read the book independently.
- Invite him or her to list questions that arise from reading.

After Reading

- Discuss the child's questions. Talk about how he or she might find answers to those questions.
- Prompt the child to think more. Ask: There are many mountains in North America. Are there mountains where you live?

Pogo Books are published by Jump!
5357 Penn Avenue South
Minneapolis, MN 55419
www.jumplibrary.com

Copyright © 2020 Jump!
International copyright reserved in all countries.
No part of this book may be reproduced in any form without written permission from the publisher.

Library of Congress Cataloging-in-Publication Data

Names: Wilkins, Veronica B., 1994- author.
Title: Explore North America / by Veronica B. Wilkins.
Description: Minneapolis, MN: Jump!, Inc., 2020.
Series: A look at continents
Includes index. | Audience: Ages 7-10
Identifiers: LCCN 2019032422 (print)
LCCN 2019032423 (ebook)
ISBN 9781645272977 (hardcover)
ISBN 9781645272984 (paperback)
ISBN 9781645272991 (ebook)
Subjects: LCSH: North America–Juvenile literature.
Classification: LCC E38.5 .W54 2020 (print)
LCC E38.5 (ebook) | DDC 970–dc23
LC record available at https://lccn.loc.gov/2019032422
LC ebook record available at https://lccn.loc.gov/2019032423

Editor: Susanne Bushman
Designer: Molly Ballanger

Photo Credits: Edmund Lowe Photography/Shutterstock, cover; Dolores Harvey/Shutterstock, 1; Nancy Anderson/Shutterstock, 3; Martin M303/Shutterstock, 4; Eastgreenlander/Shutterstock, 5; Maciej Es/Shutterstock, 6-7 (foreground); Jaroslav74/Shutterstock, 6-7 (background); BGSmith/Shutterstock, 8-9; NASA, 10-11; Che_Tina_Plant/iStock, 12; Matthias Breiter/Minden Pictures/SuperStock, 13; Neel Adsul/Shutterstock, 14-15; FotoKina/Shutterstock, 16-17tl; Minerva Studio/Shutterstock, 16-17tr; John D Sirlin/Shutterstock, 16-17bl; Dreef/iStock, 16-17br; marchello74/iStock, 18; valeriy eydlin/Shutterstock, 19; Pierre Jean Durieu/Shutterstock, 20-21; AAR Studio/Shutterstock, 23.

Printed in the United States of America at Corporate Graphics in North Mankato, Minnesota.

TABLE OF CONTENTS

CHAPTER 1

MOUNTAINS AND PLAINS

Let's explore the **continent** of North America! The Grand **Canyon** is here. It is more than one mile (1.6 kilometers) deep in some places.

Greenland is part of this continent also. It is between the Arctic and Atlantic Oceans. Much of it is covered in an **ice sheet**.

North America is in the Northern **Hemisphere**. It is north of the **equator**. It is the third largest continent.

The United States and Canada make up much of North America. Greenland is Earth's largest island. Central America and the Caribbean are **regions** in the south.

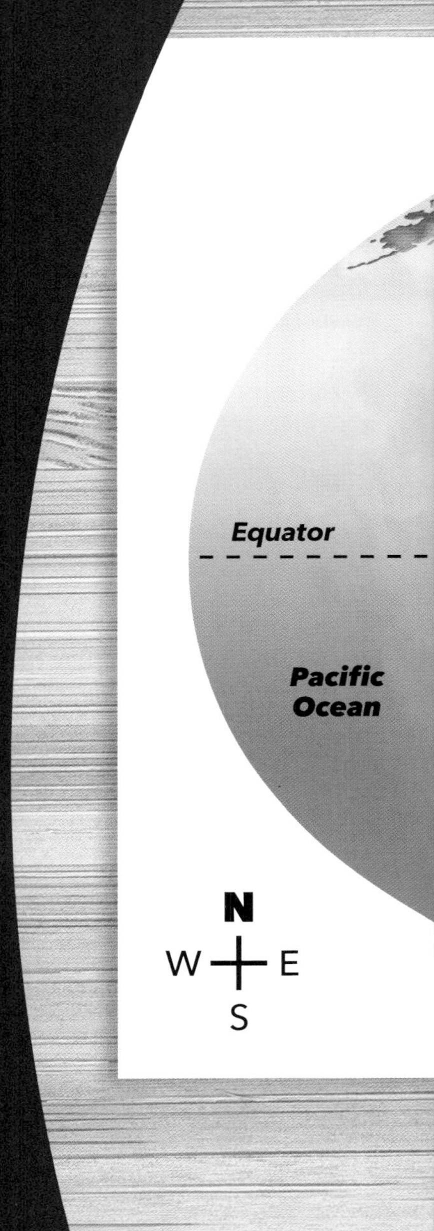

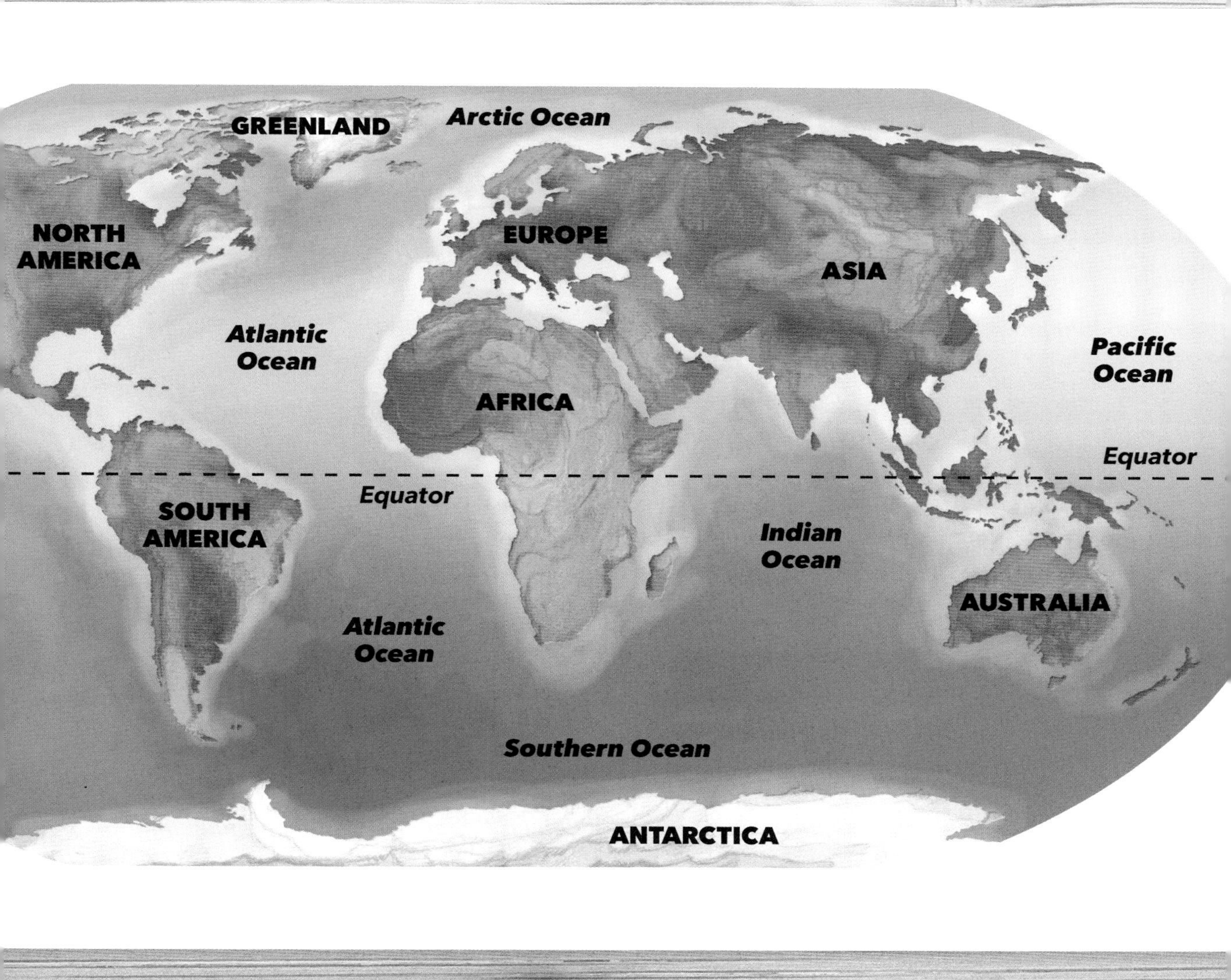
GREENLAND
Arctic Ocean
NORTH AMERICA
EUROPE
ASIA
Atlantic Ocean
Pacific Ocean
AFRICA
Equator
Equator
SOUTH AMERICA
Indian Ocean
AUSTRALIA
Atlantic Ocean
Southern Ocean
ANTARCTICA

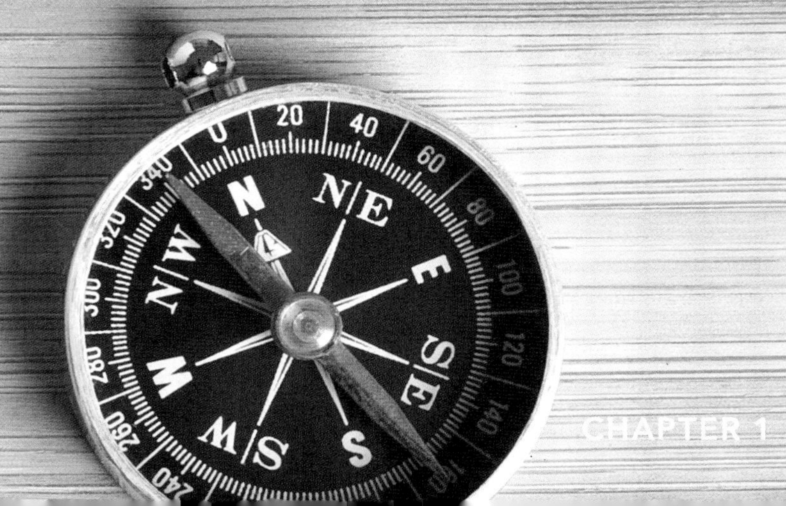

Many mountains cross this continent. The Rocky Mountains are in the West. The Appalachian Mountains are in the East. The Sierra Madres span the South.

DID YOU KNOW?

Denali is the highest peak in North America. It is 20,310 feet (6,190 meters) high. It was called Mount McKinley. But the named changed. Denali is what Native Americans called it.

Rocky Mountains

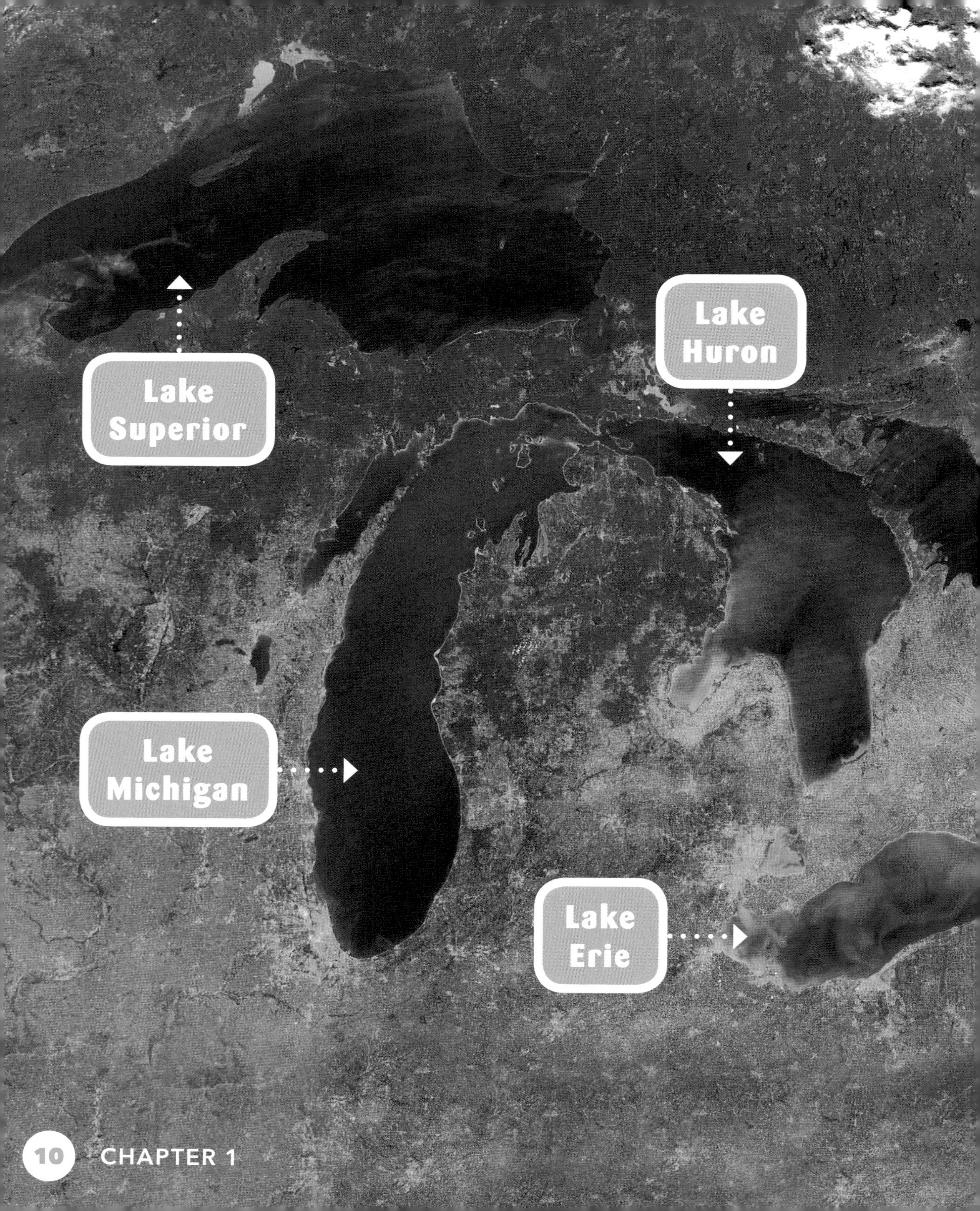

Lake Superior

Lake Huron

Lake Michigan

Lake Erie

A large **plateau** covers much of Canada. It is called the Canadian Shield. It surrounds the Hudson Bay. The five Great Lakes are below it. Lake Superior is the largest.

The Missouri and Mississippi Rivers flow through the Great **Plains**. The Mississippi River is the longest in North America. It is 2,348 miles (3,779 km) long.

WHAT DO YOU THINK?

Lake Superior formed more than one billion years ago! How? **Tectonic plates** moved apart. They could have split the continent in two! How do you think North America would be different if this had happened?

CHAPTER 2

ANIMALS AND CLIMATE

Monkeys roam the **tropical** rain forests of Central America. Green iguanas live in the trees. These lizards can grow to be 6.6 feet (2.0 m) long!

See caribou in northern Canada. Grizzly bears live in the Rocky Mountains. Their cubs are usually twins!

It is never cold in the Caribbean. Many tropical birds live here. Manatees swim in the warm waters. They eat sea grasses.

TAKE A LOOK!

There are many **climate** regions on this continent. Take a look!

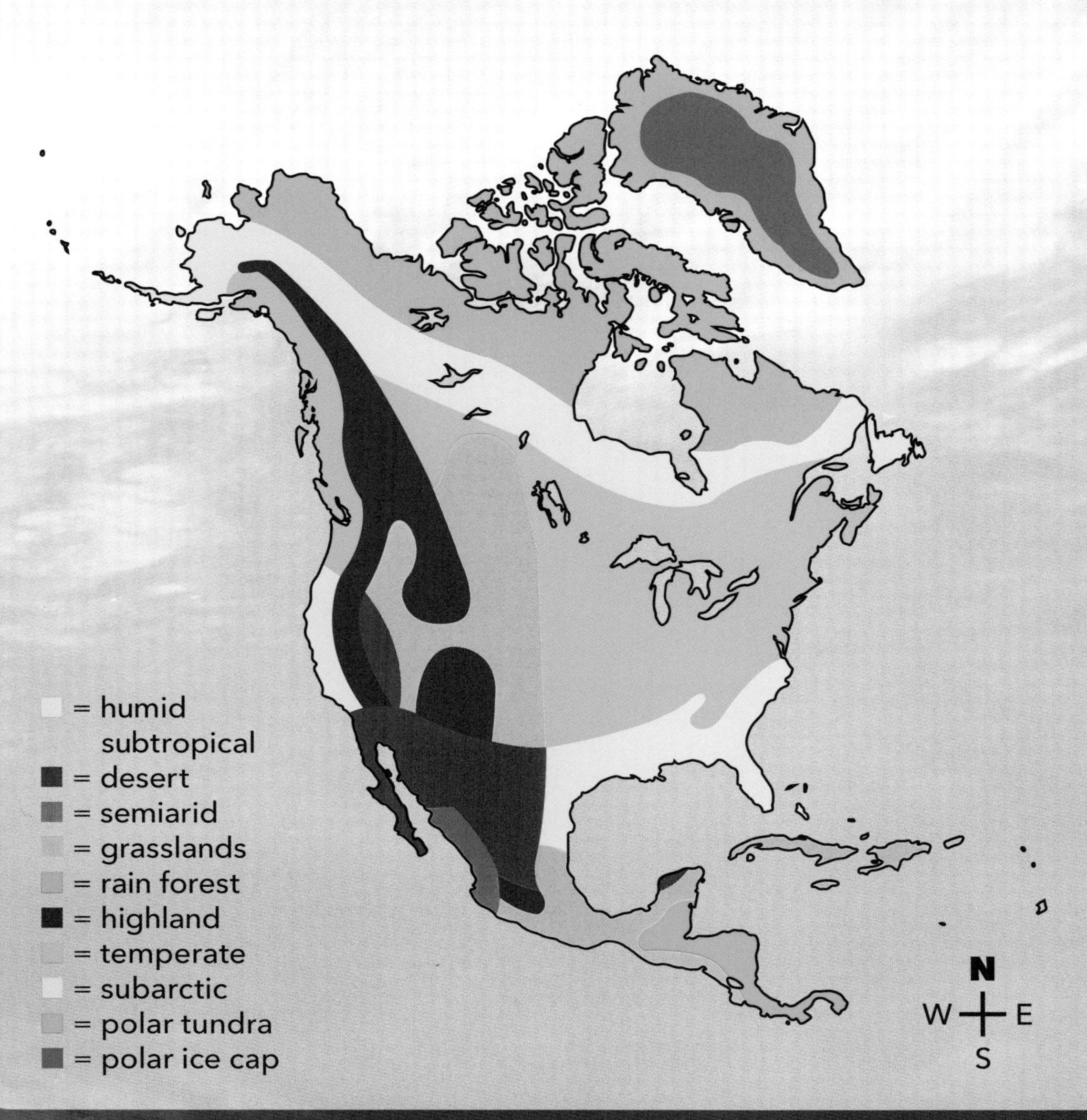

Weather changes throughout the year. From June to October, **hurricanes** can happen. Where? They hit the Gulf of Mexico and the East Coast. **Tornadoes** happen in spring and summer. Thunderstorms do, too. Winter brings snowstorms in the North.

DID YOU KNOW?

The United States has the most tornadoes of any country on Earth. They are most common from Texas to Nebraska. Some call this area Tornado Alley.

hurricane
tornado

thunderstorm

snowstorm

CHAPTER 3

LIFE IN NORTH AMERICA

Many people live by large bodies of water. Goods are carried from place to place by waterways.

Chicago, Illinois

The United States has the largest **population**. More than half of the people on this continent live here! New York City is the U.S. city with the most people.

Many **cultures** come together in North America. Native Americans celebrate their cultures through art. They dance and sing, too.

Do you live in North America? Would you like to explore more of it?

QUICK FACTS & TOOLS

AT A GLANCE

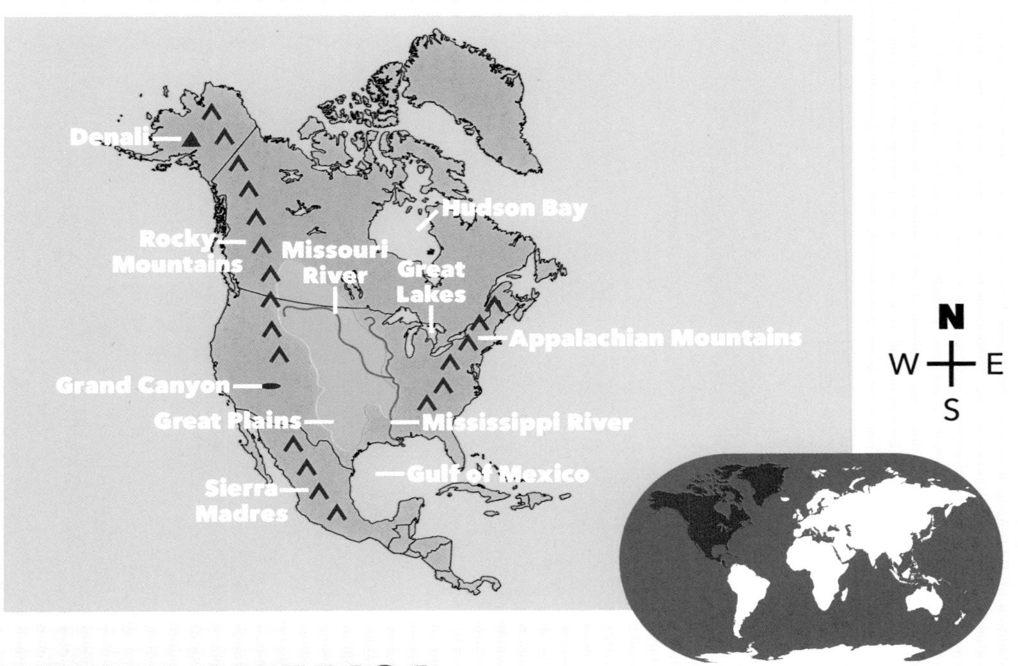

NORTH AMERICA

Size: 9,355,000 square miles (24,229,338 square km)

Size Rank: Asia, Africa, **North America**, South America, Antarctica, Europe, Australia

Population Estimate: 370 million people (2019 estimate)

Exports: Machinery, vehicles, oil

Facts: North America could fit the state of Texas nearly 35 times.

The Greenland Ice Sheet covers more than 700,000 square miles (1,812,992 square km).

GLOSSARY

canyon: A deep narrow valley with steep sides and often a river running through it.

climate: The weather typical of a certain place over a long period of time.

continent: One of the seven large landmasses of Earth.

cultures: The ideas, customs, traditions, and ways of life of groups of people.

equator: An imaginary line around the middle of Earth that is an equal distance from the North and South Poles.

hemisphere: Half of a round object, especially of Earth.

hurricanes: Violent tropical storms with heavy rains and high winds.

ice sheet: A permanent layer of ice covering a large area of land.

plains: Large, flat areas of land.

plateau: An area of level ground that is higher than the surrounding area.

population: The total number of people who live in a place.

regions: General areas or specific districts or territories.

tectonic plates: Massive, irregularly shaped slabs of rock that are deep underground and move slowly, changing Earth's landscape.

tornadoes: Violent wind storms that appear as dark, funnel-shaped clouds.

tropical: Of or having to do with the hot, rainy areas of the tropics.

INDEX

TO LEARN MORE

Finding more information is as easy as 1, 2, 3.

1. Go to www.factsurfer.com
2. Enter "exploreNorthAmerica" into the search box.
3. Choose your book to see a list of websites.